Know Your Numbers

Eggs and Legs

Counting by Twos

by Michael Dahl **illustrated by Todd Ouren**

Special thanks to our advisers for their expertise:

Stuart Farm, M.Ed., Mathematics Lecturer
University of North Dakota, Grand Forks

Susan Kesselring, M.A., Literacy Educator
Rosemount-Apple Valley-Eagan (Minnesota) School District

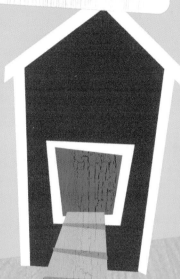

PICTURE WINDOW BOOKS
Minneapolis, Minnesota

Managing Editor: Catherine Neitge
Creative Director: Terri Foley
Art Director: Keith Griffin
Editor: Christianne Jones
Designer: Todd Ouren
Page production: Picture Window Books
The illustrations in this book were prepared digitally.

Picture Window Books
1710 Roe Crest Drive
North Mankato, MN 56003
www.capstonepub.com

Copyright © 2005 by Picture Window Books, a Capstone
imprint. All rights reserved. No part of this book may be
reproduced without written permission from the publisher.
The publisher takes no responsibility for the use of any of
the materials or methods described in this book, nor for
the products thereof.

Library of Congress Cataloging-in-Publication Data
Dahl, Michael.
Eggs and legs : counting by twos / written by Michael Dahl;
illustrated by Todd Ouren.
p. cm. — (Know your numbers)
ISBN 978-1-4048-0945-1 (hardcover)
ISBN 978-1-4048-1114-0 (paperback)
1. Counting—Juvenile literature. 2. Multiplication—Juvenile
literature. I. Ouren, Todd, ill. II. Title.

QA113.D328 2005
513.2'11—dc22   2004019004

Mrs. Hen stared at her empty nest.

Printed in the United States   6011

TWO little legs went
running into the barn.

FOUR little legs were hiding in the corn.

SIX little legs were chasing the dog.

2 4 **6**

9

EIGHT little legs were bothering a cow.

TEN little legs were climbing on the tractor.

TWELVE little legs
were playing with the pig.

FOURTEEN little legs were scurrying through the beans.

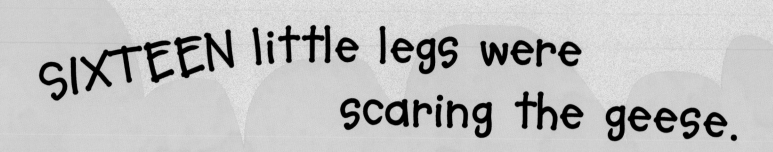

SIXTEEN little legs were scaring the geese.

2 4 6 8 10 12 14 **16**

19

EIGHTEEN little legs were scooped up by the farmer's wife.

TWENTY little legs were back in the nest.

2 4 6 8 10 12 14 16 18 **20**

"Whew!" said Mrs. Hen. "These chicks really keep me on my toes!"

Fun Facts

- A hen lays an average of 300 eggs a year.

- A mother hen turns over her eggs about 50 times a day.

- The biggest chicken egg weighed more than 1 pound (.45 kilograms).

- Most chicken eggs are either white or brown, but some chickens lay blue-green eggs.

- There are more chickens in the world than people.

- The record number of yolks found in a single egg is nine.

On the Web

FactHound offers a safe, fun way to find Web sites related to this book. All of the sites on FactHound have been researched by our staff. *www.facthound.com*

1. Visit the FactHound home page.
2. Enter a search word related to this book, or type in this special code: 1404809457
3. Click on the FETCH IT button.

Your trusty FactHound will fetch the best Web sites for you!

Find the Numbers

Now you have finished reading the story, but a surprise still awaits you. Hidden in each picture is a multiple of 2 from 2 to 20. Can you find them all?

2–the hook above the door

4–the handle of the shovel

6–on the wheelbarrow wheel

8–the pulley on the well

10–on the tractor engine

12–on the mud splash on the right page

14–above the beans on the right page

16–between the wings of the goose

18–between the four eggs on the left

20–on the bottom right eggshell

Look for all of the books in the Know Your Numbers series:

Downhill Fun
A Counting Book About Winter

Eggs and Legs
Counting By Twos

Footprints in the Snow
Counting By Twos

From the Garden
A Counting Book About Growing Food

Hands Down
Counting By Fives

Lots of Ladybugs!
Counting By Fives

On the Launch Pad
A Counting Book About Rockets

One Big Building
A Counting Book About Construction

One Checkered Flag
A Counting Book About Racing

One Giant Splash
A Counting Book About the Ocean

Pie for Piglets
Counting By Twos

Starry Arms
Counting By Fives